Teaching
10 Fabulous
Forms of Poetry

BY PAUL B. JANECZKO

SCHOLASTIC
PROFESSIONAL BOOKS

NEW YORK • TORONTO • LONDON • AUCKLAND • SYDNEY
MEXICO CITY • NEW DELHI • HONG KONG

for Bobbi Katz,

who always writes from the heart

CREDITS

Unless otherwise noted, all poems are written by the author.

Page 19, "Beatrix Potter" from *Laughing Time: Collected Nonsense* by William J. Smith. Copyright © 1990 by William J. Smith. Reprinted by permission of Farrar, Straus, & Giroux.

Page 59, "Catcher Sings the Blues" from *That Sweet Diamond: Baseball Poems* by Paul B. Janeczko. Copyright © 1998 Paul B. Janeczko. Reprinted by permission of Atheneum.

Page 60, "My Daddy" from *Nathaniel Talking* by Eloise Greenfield. Copyright © 1988 by Eloise Greenfield. Used by permission of S©ott Treimel, New York

Page 62, "A Giraffe" by Maureen W. Armour. Copyright © by Maureen W. Armour. Used by permission of the author.

Page 38, haiku by Penny Harter Copyright © 2000 by Penny Harter; haiku by J. Patrick Lewis, from *Stone Bench in an Empty Park*, edited by Paul B. Janeczko (Orchard, 2000). Copyright © by J. Patrick Lewis. Used by permission of the author; haiku by Cor van den Heuvel from *The Haiku Anthology*, third edition, edited by Cor van den Heuvel (WW. Norton, 1999). Copyright © 1999 by Cor van den Heuvel. Used by permission of the author; haiku by Anita Wintz. Copyright © 2000 by Anita Wintz. Used by permission of Marian Reiner for the author.

Cover design by Jaime Lucero
Cover art by Gil Murray
Interior design by Kathy Massaro

ISBN 0-439-07346-4
Copyright © 2000 by Paul B. Janeczko. All rights reserved.
Printed in U.S.A.

Contents

Introduction 4

Acrostics:
POEMS WITH A SPECIAL EDGE 6

Cinquain:
GETTING IN THE FLOW 13

Clerihew:
POKING FUN AT WHO'S WHO 19

Limerick:
THERE ONCE WAS A VERSE SO FUN 28

Haiku:
WORD-PAINTING IN 17 SYLLABLES 38

Senryu:
HAIKU WITH ATTITUDE 47

Tanka:
5 LINES THAT STIR THE SOUL 53

Blues Poems:
LETTING THE SPIRIT SING 59

The Ballad:
STORYTELLING IN VERSE 68

Concrete Poems:
WHEN WORDS TAKE SHAPE 79

Bonus
Lesson
Found Poems:
EDITING AT ITS EXTREME 87

Final Thoughts 95

Recommended Books on Teaching Poetry Writing 96

Introduction

When I was in grammar school (the very name gives good insight into the focus of the place), we didn't "do" poetry. Oh, we had to read the stuff, all classic and traditional poems, all rhyming poems, most tedious and beyond me. As far as *writing* poetry was concerned, we never had the chance to try. The prevailing wisdom seemed to be that it was reserved for "real" writers, i.e., inspired, erudite white guys who were, mostly, dead. Not being a particularly involved student, I imagine I was relieved. If I had trouble understanding the poems that I had to read, there was no way that I could ever dream about writing the stuff. Little did I know how much I was missing—or that poetry would later become my life's work.

Luckily for our children and our culture, things have changed. Many kids in elementary schools and middle schools have been blessed with teachers who were not satisfied with business as usual. Teachers who have embraced an approach to the profession that brings the best material and the best teaching styles to their kids. I've been fortunate to have been part of that change: first as a high school English teacher for 22 years, then as an editor of poetry anthologies, and finally, as a poet and visiting writer.

When I was teaching, it was not uncommon for a teacher to save poetry for the spring of the year, that time of year that is, supposedly, best suited for the study of poetry. I was never sure why that was. I mean, what makes April an appropriate time to read "Snowbound" or poems about apple picking, dirty snow on city streets, or football? I did get a little insight into the issue a few years back when I asked a group of teachers why they saved their poetry unit for the end of the year. They were sheepish but candid in their response: if they didn't get to the poetry unit, it wouldn't be a big loss. I was stunned by this admission, but after giving it some thought, I realized that their answer addressed their real concern: they felt uncomfortable teaching poetry reading and writing. They *want* to teach poetry. On some level they realize that poetry is important—but they are not sure how to "do" poetry.

I've always been a firm believer that poetry is far too important to be left for a mammoth end-of-the-year unit, but virtually ignored the rest of the year. Poetry is life. And we need to live life every day, not save it for the spring.

I hope this book will help you bring poetry writing into your classroom on a regular basis. There are no monster units outlined in the book. Rather, it is a careful look at 10 types of poetry that your students will enjoy writing. Each poetic form is supported by a sequence of reproducible worksheets that guide students through the process of writing a poem. Photocopy and use them any way you wish, guiding students through them or handing them out for students to have fun with entirely on their own. Each lesson begins with a reproducible poetry page featuring a few examples of the poetic form explored. This page is followed by background information and teaching suggestions for each worksheet. Taken together, the student worksheets provide children with the scaffolding they may need as they plan, draft, and revise their work.

At first blush, some of these forms may seem beyond the skills of your students. Although you obviously know your students better than I do, I would not give up on giving them the chance to try to write some of the more sophisticated ones. I have arranged the poems in rough order of sophistication. I suggest that you work your way through this book in the order I have suggested. In that way, the success your students have with some of the easier forms might very well give them (and you!) the confidence to tackle the more demanding forms later in the year.

And, I think we've all had the experience of having our students pleasantly surprise us by accomplishing something that we were not sure they could handle. Perhaps we need to give young writers the benefit of the doubt.

We need to develop a classroom atmosphere in which students are encouraged to try new things. To experiment rather to settle for the comfort of doing the "same old thing" well. They are not going to succeed all the time. No one does. But the kids need to know that it's okay if they try something daring and the results are not what they had hoped for. Perhaps in the attempt they learn something to do differently the next time. But we must always support students when they take risks.

Although it should go without saying that you ought to take a crack at any writing assignment—prose or poetry—you give your students, I will say it: you should take a crack at any writing assignment—prose or poetry—that you give your students. On a very practical level, it will give you a chance to work out the bugs you might discover in an assignment of your own design. And with activities such as the ones in this book, it will allow you to discover areas that might give your students difficulty and require different examples, more explanations, or general tweaking to meet the needs of your students.

Another strategy to consider, particularly with longer poems or difficult forms, is allowing students to work with other students to write collaborative poems. Your kids can work with one other student or they can each supply a few lines for a class poem. Such collaborative efforts can help develop a sense of community among the students in your class. It can also help build a young poet's confidence.

TARZAN

Tan
Athletic
Resourceful
Zooms
Assertive
Nimble

EMMA

Eager to learn
Makes time to read
Marvelous artist
Adores her white poodle

CAT

Can't
Avoid
Trouble

TRASH

Takes a
Really
Astounding
Stomach to
Handle this mess.

Teaching 10 Fabulous Forms of Poetry by Paul B. Janeczko   Scholastic Professional Books

Acrostics:

POEMS WITH A SPECIAL EDGE

The acrostic is an ancient poetic form. The word "acrostic" comes from the Greek *akrostikhis: akron*, end + *stikhos*, line. You can find acrostic poems in ancient Greek and Latin literature. In addition, some of the Old Testament Psalms were written in Hebrew as acrostic poems. Since that time, many authors have written acrostic poems, including British writer Geoffrey Chaucer and master storyteller Edgar Allen Poe. In the traditional acrostic, the first letter of each line spells a word or phrase, most often the title or subject of the poem. Poe went the traditional acrostic one better, however, when he wrote "A Valentine to _____." The name of his friend Frances Sargeant Osgood was spelled out by taking the first letter of the first line, the second letter of the second line, and so on, throughout the 21-line poem. Here are the first seven lines of the poem, with the letters spelling out "Frances" in bold print:

> **F**or her this rhyme is penned, whose luminous eyes,
> B**r**ightly expressive as the twins of Laeda,
> Sh**a**ll find her own sweet name, that, nestling lies
> Upo**n** the page, enwrapped from every reader.
> Sear**c**h narrowly the lines!—they hold a treasure
> Divin**e**—a talisman—an amulet
> That mu**st** be worn at heart. Search well the measure—

There are several ways to write an acrostic poem. It can be a list, with a different item or characteristic (trait) on each line. "Emma" is a list poem made up of phrases; "Tarzan" is a list poem made up of single words. Or, an acrostic poem can comprise a statement or question that works its way through the poem, as in the examples "Cat" and "Trash." The two approaches can also be combined.

Acrostic poems are quite simple, and they are a great way to encourage students to write poetry. Writing acrostic poems helps young writers begin to think about finding the right word for a particular spot in a poem, even though the right words in an acrostic poem are determined, to some degree, by the letters of the word chosen as the subject of the poem.

Writing An Acrostic

All poems need the "right words" and the acrostic poem is a good way to introduce this concept. Students gain experience with word choice as they look for the right word to fit the letters of the subject of their poems.

Thinking About Yourself

Before you tell students that they will be writing an acrostic poem about themselves, ask them to fill out their "Personal Inventory" (REPRODUCIBLE #1, page 10) as honestly as possible. They won't need a lot of time, maybe 10–15 minutes. Knowing that time is limited should help them focus on the task at hand. It is important that students know that what they write on this page is completely private. No one in the class will read what they write, unless they decide to make it public.

Ask students to write words and phrases, thoughts and feelings, in the boxes provided on this worksheet. Let them know that you do not expect them to write a poem about these ideas, but that you hope they'll include some of the

Paul

Who am I?

Likes/Dislikes		Personality
· Good food · Baseball! · Jazz · a good walk · Summer in Maine	Carelessness · Bad drivers · injustice · long lines · water in the cellar · bad TV · college sports	· funny / serious · Thoughtful · self-critic · hard for me to relax

Treasures	Dreams & Plans
· family photos · computer disks · special books · momentos from friends	· Keep writing · watch Emma grow · watch as much baseball as I can · Keep growing as a person

Physical Characteristics	Family
· full, bushy beard · lots of silver in my hair · green eyes · glasses · about 5'10" · left ear pierced · loud voice	· 2 brothers + 1 sister · still in touch w/ them all · Emma, 10-year-old daughter · Nadine, my wife · Rose, our white standard poodle · a handful of tropical fish

rich personal material in their poem—whatever they wish to share. They don't even have to write sentences. The point of the exercise is to get them to write information quickly before they have time to weigh their words and fuss over spelling.

Finding the Right Details

After students have filled out the "Personal Inventory" on REPRODUCIBLE #1, give them a few minutes to read through what they've written. They may want to make some last minute additions. Hand out REPRODUCIBLE #2, ("Finding the Right Details" page 11) on which students underline the most important information, then write some details in the space provided.

The worksheet will also help them discover if their selections have anything in common. They might notice that many of them are connected to some passion in their lives, such as music, baseball, ballet. They may choose to write an acrostic poem about themselves using that interest as a unifying theme for the poem.

Starting Your First Draft

Even though an acrostic poem can be written about anything—that's part of their appeal to young writers—I've found it's best if students write their first acrostic poems about themselves. The final reproducible (#3, page 12) asks students to begin drafting their poems. Although I suggest they begin their draft by writing the letters of their name down the left hand edge of the worksheet, please make sure they don't simply look at those letters and try to think of words to fit them. This is too limiting; poetry is about possibilities, not limitations. Rather, your students should concentrate on finding a way to work some of their key, favorite details into poetic lines beginning with those letters.

Since an acrostic poem can be written as a list as well as a statement or question, the second part of the reproducible asks students to write an acrostic poem that is not the form they used in their first try. After students have had a chance to write both types of acrostics, take some time to discuss how they felt about each type. Was one easier than the other? Why? Did they like writing one type more than the other? Why?

RESOURCES

Autumn: An Alphabet Acrostic (Houghton Mifflin, 1997) and *Spring: An Alphabet Acrostic* (Houghton Mifflin, 1999), both by Stephen Schnur, abound with well-crafted acrostic poems and rich illustrations.

Name _____ Date _____

Personal Inventory

In the spaces below, write down information about yourself.

Likes/Dislikes	**Dreams/Plans**
Personality	**Physical Characteristics**
Material Treasures	**Family and Family Life**

Teaching 10 Fabulous Forms of Poetry by Paul B. Janeczko   Scholastic Professional Books

Name _____ Date _____

Finding the Right Details

1 Look at the words and phrases you used to describe yourself and your interests on worksheet 1. Underline those you feel are most important. Are there any that reveal a side of you that other people might not know? List them in the space below. Such details are called "telling details," meaning they tell or reveal something about someone or thing, and all good writing needs them.

◎ _____

◎ _____

◎ _____

◎ _____

◎ _____

◎ _____

2 As you look at your personal inventory sheet and the items you listed above, do you notice anything these things have in common? For example, some of the things you feel are important about you might be related to friends or family, your pet, sports, or school. You might want to use a theme to unify your poem. If you had to choose one word to describe yourself, what would it be? Write it here.

_____

You don't have to use this word in your poem, but it may give you an idea for it.

Name _____ Date _____

Starting Your First Draft

1 Once you've selected your details, you are ready to start a first draft of your acrostic. Write the letters of your name down the dotted line at right. Then begin your acrostic, looking for a way to work the things you've listed in "Finding the Right Details" into the poem.

2 When you have finished your draft, write another draft on the same subject (in the space at right), but this time make it a different kind of acrostic. If the poem above is a list, make this one a statement or question about you. Take another look at the sample poems so you can see how these two kinds of acrostic poems work.

3 After you have drafted two versions of the acrostic poem, decide which one you prefer. Underline the parts in that poem you especially like. Try to rework your drafts into poems you like enough to read to your friends.

Teaching 10 Fabulous Forms of Poetry by Paul B. Janeczko   Scholastic Professional Books

Cinquain

Pink sky
turns to purple
as the sun slides behind
the mountains and day slowly turns
to night.

Stillness
of night deepens:
stars are scattered across
black velvet sky in glorious
array.

Snowflakes
dance in the square
of light from a window
as a man sits, quiet and still,
and waits.

Oh, cat
are you grinning
curled in the window seat
as sun warms you this December
morning?

Teaching 10 Fabulous Forms of Poetry by Paul B. Janeczko   Scholastic Professional Books

The Cinquain:

GETTING IN THE FLOW

A poet named Adelaide Crapsey invented the cinquain in 1911, three years before her death from tuberculosis at the age of 36. Ill much of her life, she didn't live to see her own cinquains published. However, her poetic legacy has been enjoyed by many teachers and young writers.

Deriving its name from *quinque*, the Latin word for "five," the cinquain is a poem of five lines. Like the haiku and the tanka, the cinquain follows a pattern based on syllable count. There are 22 syllables in a cinquain, distributed among the five lines in a specific pattern: 2, 4, 6, 8, 2.

A good cinquain will flow smoothly, like a haiku. If a cinquain sounds like it is five distinct thoughts with a pause after each, the poet has missed the point. In a cinquain, the poet tries to create a complete thought, whether it's a powerful image or a feeling. Usually a sentence or two, rather than a list of disjointed phrases, the poem should flow, building toward a conclusion. It must not simply stop because the poet has used up the allotted number of syllables. Like some other poems—the haiku and tanka, for example—the spirit of the cinquain is more important than sticking to a syllable count at the expense of the images and feelings in the poem.

Writing a Cinquain

Students can begin their work by studying the structure of cinquains. Before they get started, you'll want to make copies of page 13 (the model poems page) to distribute. Read one or two of the poems aloud, then encourage volunteers to read. Ask your students what they notice. They will surely point out that the cinquains don't rhyme. They may also notice that the first four lines get progressively longer, but the final line is quite short. Others might even discern that each poem has a noun in the opening line. Give your students a chance to share their observations with the class.

Looking at Cinquains

After you've talked about the poems, hand out REPRODUCIBLE #1 (page 16), which asks students to look closely at cinquains, first by counting the syllables in each line. Once the students have marked and counted the syllables in each poem, ask them if they see a pattern. They should note that, except for the third line of the last poem, the cinquains follow a precise syllable count: 2, 4, 6, 8, 2. You might want to work through one poem with them on the board. The second part of "Looking at Cinquains" asks students to explore the language of the poem by underlining sensory words, to spot the central image in the poem, and to explain briefly how the poem makes them feel. By the time students have completed the worksheet, they should have a sense of the structure and spirit of a cinquain.

Picturing a Scene for Your Cinquain

REPRODUCIBLE #2 (page 17) presents a web for students to fill in as they explore a scene or object that they would like to include in their own cinquains. The subject of their poems can be real—like the snowman in the schoolyard or the sunset reflecting off their apartment building—or it can come from their imagination. You might provide some evocative photographs, art prints, or print ads with interesting pictures to spur their imaginations. As students fill in the web and prepare to write a draft, remind them that they need not include everything from their web in the poem. A thoughtfully completed web may, in fact, provide enough material for several poems. When students are satisfied with their webs, they can draft their cinquains on a separate sheet. At right are two of my webs to share with your students:

Looking at Your Draft

Drafting several different poems written in the same form definitely helps young writers. And after your students have had time to draft a cinquain—*or two or three*—you should probably give them several copies of REPRODUCIBLE #3, a checklist of things to look for as they edit and revise their poems. Students need ample time to use the checklist on their own poem and on a poem written by a writing partner. They should then discuss together what they wrote on their checklists and how it will affect their final drafts. Invite students to share something they learned from the process with the entire class.

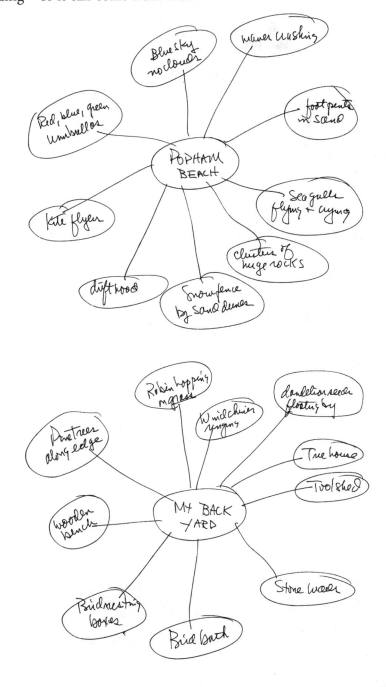

Name _____ Date _____

Looking at Cinquains

1 After you reread the sample cinquains,

◎ mark off the syllables in each line;

◎ write the number of syllables at the end of each line;

◎ determine how many syllables are in each poem.

2 For each poem, underline all the sensory words, then complete the following:

Poem 1

1. What is the central image in this poem? _____

2. How does the poem make you feel? _____

3. Circle any word that helps create this feeling.

Poem 2

1. What is the central image in this poem? _____

2. How does the poem make you feel? _____

3. Circle any word that helps create this feeling.

Poem 3

1. What is the central image in this poem? _____

2. How does the poem make you feel? _____

3. Circle any word that helps create this feeling.

Poem 4

1. What is the central image in this poem? _____

2. How does the poem make you feel? _____

3. Circle any word that helps create this feeling.

Teaching 10 Fabulous Forms of Poetry by Paul B. Janeczko   Scholastic Professional Books

Name _____ Date _____

Picturing a Scene for Your Cinquain

Your cinquain should have a central image. You may want to use a scene or an object that you can actually observe and take notes on. Or, you can imagine a scene or object and note what your imagination creates. In either case, use the web below to record your impressions. When you have filled the web with good sensory words—and you should feel free to add more "spokes" to the web—use these words to help you draft your cinquain on a separate sheet of paper.

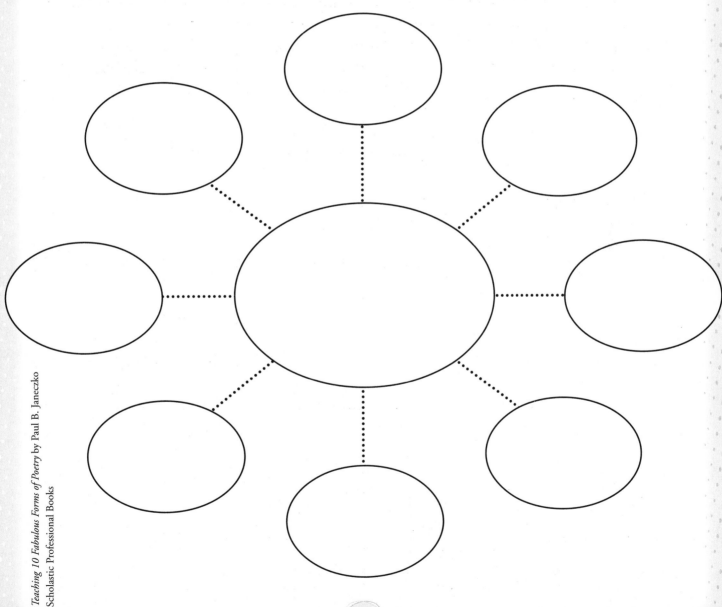

Name _____ Date _____

Looking at Your Draft

After you have written a draft you like, use this page to help you evaluate your cinquain. You may also ask a friend to help you evaluate your poem, using this same checklist.

◎ **Line Count:** How many lines in your poem? _____

◎ **Syllable Count:** How many syllables in each line of your poem? _____

◎ **Details:** Circle the specific details in your poem and list them here:

_____

_____

_____

_____

◎ **Central Image:** In a word or two, describe the central image of your cinquain:

_____ .

◎ **Favorite Words:** Underline the words in your poem that you especially like and list them here:

_____   _____   _____

_____   _____   _____

◎ **Feeling:** In a word or two, describe the overall feeling you hope your poem will give a reader.

_____

Teaching 10 Fabulous Forms of Poetry by Paul B. Janeczko   Scholastic Professional Books

Clerihew

Harry Potter
Was a magical plotter.
At Hogwarts he became a master
After many a goof and disaster

Mark Twain
Wrote books in a humorous vein
His characters can make us **grin,**
Especially that rascal Huck Finn.

Edgar Alan Poe
Penned stories that we all know
And every one that he wrote
Seems to end on a gruesome note.

Beatrix Potter,
While doodling with her pen on a **fuzzy blotter,**
May well have developed the habit
Of drawing Peter Rabbit.

—*William Jay Smith*

Teaching 10 Fabulous Forms of Poetry by Paul B. Janeczko   Scholastic Professional Books

The Clerihew:

POKING FUN AT WHO'S WHO

The clerihew was invented during the Victorian era by an English schoolboy named Edmund Clerihew Bentley. The boy went on to become a well-regarded writer and creator of the classic locked-room mystery, *Trent's Last Case*. However, Bentley will always be known as the creator of the clerihew, a short form of light verse that he introduced in *Biography for Beginners* by "E. Clerihew" (1905), widely imitated by W.H. Auden in his book *Academic Graffiti*. Bentley included many of his clerihews in a column he wrote for a London newspaper during World War II.

A clerihew is a four-line poem about a celebrity. It is made up of two rhymed couplets, giving it a rhyme scheme of *aabb*. It gently pokes fun at the subject, and you may need to emphasize this with your students so their poems do not turn out to be hurtful. A clerihew often includes some reflection on the person's fame. In the sample poems, for example, you can see Harry Potter's goofs and Poe's obsession with writing gruesome poems and stories.

One thing that makes the clerihew challenging is that it must include the celebrity's name at the end of the first line, which means you need to rhyme it. (You might want to remind your students that it's usually easier to rhyme a one- or two-syllable word.) I often permit young writers to include a few words of explanation before the subject's name, i.e., "Cubs slugger, Sammy Sosa," or "Pop singer, Jewel." A true clerihew, like the sample poems, does not use this technique, but young writers sometimes feel more comfortable with this sort of opening line. I do not, however, allow them to write something like, "There once was famous director named Spielberg." That's not a suitable opening line for a clerihew.

Provide students with this checklist for a good clerihew:

- A clerihew is always four lines long, written in two couplets.
- It is about a celebrity.
- It pokes gentle fun at the person, much like a political cartoon.
- The subject's name must be at the end of the first line (and the second line must rhyme with it).

Writing a Clerihew

Although a clerihew is about a celebrity, it asks that the students look carefully at the person and find one characteristic that can be the basis for a humorous poem. In your pre-writing discussions, explore the issue of "what makes a celebrity," illuminating characteristics of famous people. Make a list of celebrities' memorable habits or traits (Liz Taylor's marriages, Michael Jordan's money, a President's pet, and so forth).

Looking at the Clerihew

Since the clerihew is a poetic form that is probably new to your students, it is a good idea to make sure they understand what goes into a good clerihew. REPRODUCIBLE #1 (pages 23–24) gives them the chance to read the poems carefully and note some of the elements of the form. This worksheet will be most effective if you let each student work on his/her own, then allow time for a class discussion of what students discover about the form.

Before you hand out REPRODUCIBLE #1 ("Looking at the Clerihew"), read one of the clerihew on page 19 aloud to the class. Write it on the board or use an overhead projector film so the whole class can see it. Ask students what they notice about the poem. Their responses and discussion should help them when working on this worksheet.

Finding a Subject

Before students can write a good clerihew, they need to come up with a good subject. Begin the brainstorming process by asking students for categories of celebrities (e.g., TV stars, musicians, historical figures). REPRODUCIBLE #2 (pages 25–26) allows them to record some of the categories of celebrities that are important to them. Next, have students write a few specific names under each category, encouraging them to go beyond Hollywood and athletic celebrities. Remind them that they can use historical and literary figures in their poems, as in the sample poems. Since factual information is part of a good clerihew, students may be able to incorporate something they've learned in art or social studies or science. Researching a historical figure before writing a poem would be a good homework assignment.

Once students have generated lists of subjects, have them select one. Next, they should list some things that come to mind when they think of this person. They might include aspects of that person's behavior, physical appearance, or a word or two about his/her accomplishments. Students should look for one significant thing to poke fun at in their poem.

Before they use their information to begin drafting their clerihew, give your students a chance to share their lists with the class and ask for feedback and suggestions.

RESOURCES

E.C. Bentley. *The Complete Clerihews of E. Clerihew Bentley.* Oxford University Press, 1982. Among the many "very British" poems, you will find good examples that will work for American students.

Final Copy Checklist

While students are working on their poems, you should take the opportunity to circulate around the room. Spend some time checking in with each student. When you find something that is noteworthy—even an enthusiastic attitude or good effort—celebrate it. Ask a few students if they would like to read their drafts to the class, or ask if you can read a few aloud. Nothing encourages young writers more than having their good work acknowledged or read aloud to the class.

When students feel they are ready to work on their final draft, hand out REPRODUCIBLE #3 (page 27), a final copy checklist. Go over the worksheet with them to make sure they know and understand the three items they need to check before writing a final draft. And remind them to use the sample poems as a reference, too.

Name _____ Date _____

Looking at the Clerihew

Carefully read through the sample clerihews and see if you can spot what the poems have in common. Write your observations in the spaces below.

Poem 1

1. What is the subject of the poem? _____

2. How many lines are in the poem? _____

3. Write the words that rhyme in the poem. _____
_____

4. Draw arrows connecting the lines that rhyme. Is there a pattern (or rhyme scheme)? _____

5. Can you find anything humorous in the poem? Jot down the humorous words and ideas you see. _____
_____
_____.

Poem 2

1. What is the subject of the poem? _____

2. How many lines are in the poem? _____

3. Write the words that rhyme in the poem. _____
_____

4. Draw arrows connecting the lines that rhyme. Is there a pattern (or rhyme scheme)? _____

5. Can you find anything humorous in the poem? Jot down the humorous words and ideas you see. _____
_____
_____.

Poem 3

1. What is the subject of the poem? _____

2. How many lines are in the poem? _____

3. Write the words that rhyme in the poem. _____

_____

4. Draw arrows connecting the lines that rhyme. Is there a pattern (or rhyme scheme)? _____

5. Can you find anything humorous in the poem? Jot down the humorous words and ideas you see. _____

_____

_____

_____ .

Poem 4

1. What is the subject of the poem? _____

2. How many lines are in the poem? _____

3. Write the words that rhyme in the poem. _____

_____

4. Draw arrows connecting the lines that rhyme. Is there a pattern (or rhyme scheme)? _____

5. Can you find anything humorous in the poem? Jot down the humorous words and ideas you see. _____

_____

_____

_____ .

Teaching 10 Fabulous Forms of Poetry by Paul B. Janeczko   Scholastic Professional Books

Name _____ Date _____

Finding a Subject

1 List four categories of celebrities or noteworthy people that interest you. Keep in mind that you can choose historical or literary celebrities as well as contemporary Hollywood-types. Then, list a few people that come to mind in each category.

1. _____

◎ _____

◎ _____

◎ _____

2. _____

◎ _____

◎ _____

◎ _____

3. _____

◎ _____

◎ _____

◎ _____

4. _____

◎ _____

◎ _____

◎ _____

2 Circle a favorite person on each list.

3 Write the name of the person you think will make the best subject for your clerihew here:

_____

4 List a few things that come to mind when you think of this person:

◎ _____

◎ _____

◎ _____

◎ _____

◎ _____

5 Is there something about this person that is easy to poke fun at? Write it here:

_____

_____

_____

_____

_____

_____

When you've finished this worksheet, try drafting your clerihew. Don't forget to look at the poems on page 19 if you're not sure how your poem should look and sound.

Teaching 10 Fabulous Forms of Poetry by Paul B. Janeczko   Scholastic Professional Books

Name _____ Date _____

Checklist for Final Copy

Before you write your final copy, answer these questions:

1 Are there two couplets in your poem? Check the words at the end of each line. Do the words at the end of lines one and two sound alike? Do the same thing for lines three and four. Write your rhyming words below:

line 1 _____

line 2 _____

line 3 _____

line 4 _____

2 Does your poem have a lighthearted tone, or does it sound mean? Jot down words that show that the poem is meant to be playful. Change any words that seem mean.

_____

_____

_____

_____

_____

_____

3 Read your clerihew out loud to a friend. Listen for the rhythm. If the poem sounds choppy or awkward, see if you can find the reason for this and fix it. It might only mean changing a word or two.

The Limerick

There once was a girl named Maureen
Who wished she were skinny and lean
But she loved pizza pie,
Pastrami on rye,
And ate till her plate was clean.

A lady who loved the trombone
Was lucky she lived all alone.
When she started to play,
Her friends stayed away,
And left her to sputter and moan.

There once was a poodle named Rose
Who liked to dance on her toes.
She twirled and she spun,
Had barrels of fun,
Until she fell on her nose

—*Emma Janeczko*

There once was a girl named Ann
Who wanted to buy a fan.
She skipped to the store
And dashed through the door,
Where she tripped and fell in a pan.

—*Emma Janeczko*

Teaching 10 Fabulous Forms of Poetry by Paul B. Janeczko   Scholastic Professional Books

Limericks by Edward Lear

There was an old man who said, "Well!
Will *nobody* answer this bell?
    I have pulled day and night
    Till my hair has turned white,
But nobody answers the bell!"

        There was an Old Man in a tree,
        Whose Whiskers were lovely to see;
           But the Birds of the Air
           Pluck'd them perfectly bare,
        To make themselves Nests in that Tree.

There was an Old Lady whose folly
Induced her to sit in a holly;
    Whereupon, by a thorn
    Her dress being torn,
She quickly became melancholy

        There was a Young Lady whose eyes
        Were unique as to color and size;
           When she opened them wide,
           People all turned aside,
        And started away in surprise.

Teaching 10 Fabulous Forms of Poetry by Paul B. Janeczko   Scholastic Professional Books

The Limerick:

THERE ONCE WAS A VERSE SO FUN...

Although Edward Lear (1812–1888) is responsible for popularizing the limerick, there is some doubt about exactly where the form came from. Some historians believe that Irish soldiers returning from France to their hometown of Limerick brought the poems home more than a hundred years before Lear was born. Limericks were included in *Mother Goose for Children,* a nursery rhyme collection published in 1719. But regardless of the origins of the form, Lear's name will always be warmly associated with the limerick. He included many of his limericks in *A Book of Nonsense,* published in 1864.

The limerick is a five-line poem, whose third and fourth lines are shorter than the other lines. Specifically, lines 1, 2, and 5 have three "feet" or stressed syllables, while lines 3 and 4 have only two. The metrical feet used in a limerick are iambic ($\cup/$), like the words *today* and *surprise,* and anapestic ($\cup\cup/$), like the words **understand** and *introduce.* The rhyme scheme for a limerick is *aabba.* The general plan for the meter goes like this (each "da da DA" is a foot):

> da da DA da da DA da da DA
> da da DA da da DA da da DA
> da da DA da da DA
> da da DA da da DA
> da da DA da da DA da da DA

Writing A Limerick

Because of the rhythm and rhyme of a limerick, they always seem to wind up being funny, even though there is nothing that prevents you from trying to write a serious limerick. In fact, writing a serious limerick is an interesting assignment for students after they have written a few light-hearted ones.

Looking at Syllables

The limerick is a poetic form that relies heavily on rhythm and rhyme. While young writers usually have little difficulty with rhyme, capturing the rhythm of a limerick is more difficult. REPRODUCIBLE #1 ("Looking at Syllables," pages 32–33) gives students a chance to tune their ears to stressed and unstressed (or accented and unaccented) syllables in words and phrases. In the handout, I identify the four most common metrical feet in English poetry and provide examples of each. I don't do this so students can memorize the names and be ready for a quiz on them, but because these metrical feet are an important part of a limerick, and of other forms of poetry, including the blues poem (see page 59).

You might want to augment the list on #1 (page 33) with words of your own, or words the students supply. Ask students to read some words aloud and deliberately accent the wrong syllables. How do these words sound now? You might also experiment with stringing together five iambic words or five anapestic words. Can your students hear the difference in the lists? Note that poets often move words around and substitute other words to get a certain rhythm in a line of poetry.

Feeling the Rhythm

Manipulating words and rhythm is a good way to introduce REPRODUCIBLE #2 (pages 34–35), which asks students to mark the stressed and unstressed syllables in four limericks. As students work on this activity, remind them that there are often variations in metrical poetry. Not every limerick, for example, will have all the proper stressed and unstressed syllables. The important thing is that your students hear and feel the rhythm of the limerick. It has an unmistakable flow or bounce. It is this flow that your students must try to incorporate into their limericks.

Drafting the Limerick

On "Drafting Your Limerick" (REPRODUCIBLE #3, page 36), I suggest that students begin with *There once was a boy/girl named* _____, or *There once was a boy/girl from* _____. These are classic opening lines that set the rhythm flowing and will surely help them get started. Of course, students should be free to work with a first line of their own choosing.

As students begin to brainstorm ideas for their limericks, remind them to think of a limerick as a *very* short story. Read aloud the limericks on pages 28–29 and ask your students if they can see how each one tells a story about a character. Early in each poem we learn about the character. We may see him or her in action before the end of the poem, when something happens to the character. Seeing each limerick as a short story might help your students draft their own poems.

RESOURCES

For more information about Edward Lear, read *That Singular Person Called Lear* (a good opening limerick line, by the way), by Susan Chitty (Atheneum, 1989). *Edward Lear's Nonsense Omnibus* (Penguin, 1986) contains all the original poems, stories, and illustrations from Lear's books.

Name _____ Date _____

Looking at Syllables

All the words we use in writing and speaking have syllables that we stress or accent. For example, in *birthday* and *water*, we stress the first syllable. In *today* and *apart* we stress the second syllable. We also stress certain syllables in longer words. *Elephant* has a stressed syllable followed by two unstressed syllables. *Understand* is the opposite: two unstressed syllables followed by a stressed syllable. We also stress certain syllables in phrases. Two or more syllables in a word or a phrase is called a foot. Poets use several different kinds of feet to give their poems rhythm:

iambic foot (∪/): today, apart

trochaic foot (/∪): pretty, sunny

anapestic foot (∪∪/): understand, disagree

dactylic foot (/∪∪): elephant, syllable

When you write rhythmical rhyming poetry, you must choose words with the stresses on the right syllables or your rhythm will be thrown off. For the most part, short rhyming verse, such as the limerick, is written with words and phrases made up of anapestic or iambic feet. It's not really important to remember the names of the feet. What is important is being able to *hear* the stressed syllables and then make sure your poem has stressed syllables in the proper places.

Before we take a closer look at a particular form of the limerick, examine the words on page 33. On the line to the right of each word, break the word into syllables and put an accent mark above the syllable that is stressed in that word. Follow the example given.

Teaching 10 Fabulous Forms of Poetry by Paul B. Janeczko   Scholastic Professional Books

Word	Stressed And Unstressed Syllables	Word	Stressed And Unstressed Syllables
example	ĕx ám plĕ	generous	
tornado		urbane	
stockade		circus	
batter		witty	
release		rotund	
narrative		skinny	
opposite		bookish	
rhythm		stunning	
carelessly		frugal	
betray		talkative	

Now choose a few of your own words to do. Try words that describe character traits, since many limericks describe people.

Word	Stressed And Unstressed Syllables	Word	Stressed And Unstressed Syllables

Teaching 10 Fabulous Forms of Poetry by Paul B. Janeczko
Scholastic Professional Books

Name _____ Date _____

Feeling the Rhythm

How are stressed and unstressed syllables used in writing limericks?

1 Read this limerick and notice the stressed and the unstressed syllables:

⌣ / ⌣ ⌣ / ⌣ ⌣ /
There once was a girl named Maureen

⌣ / ⌣ ⌣ / ⌣ ⌣ /
Who wished she were skinny and lean

⌣ ⌣ / ⌣ ⌣ /
But she loved pizza pie,

⌣ ⌣ / ⌣ /
Pastrami on rye

⌣ / ⌣ ⌣ / ⌣ /
And ate till her plate was clean.

2 Read the limericks on page 35 to yourself and then out loud. Mark the stressed and unstressed syllables. Remember, the long lines should have three stressed syllables; the short lines should have two.

Teaching 10 Fabulous Forms of Poetry by Paul B. Janeczko   Scholastic Professional Books

There once was a boy named Drew

On candy he'd chomp and he'd chew

To brush he forgot

His teeth started to rot

And now he just has a few.

A lady who loved the trombone

Was lucky she lived all alone.

When she started to play,

Her friends stayed away

And left her to sputter and moan.

There once was a poodle name Rose

Who liked to dance on her toes.

She twirled and she spun,

Had barrels of fun,

Until she fell on her nose.

Teaching 10 Fabulous Forms of Poetry by Paul B. Janeczko   Scholastic Professional Books

Name _____ **Date** _____

Drafting Your Limerick

Now it's your turn to write a limerick.

1 If you need help getting started, you might try one of these opening lines: *There once was a boy/girl named* _____ *, or There once was a boy/girl from* _____.

2 Once you have your first line, brainstorm a few rhyming words for the next line.

3 Next, look over your list of words that rhyme and see how you can make some of them part of your poem. Remember, a limerick is really a very short story, so anything you include must make sense and help tell that story. In other words, don't use a line simply because it rhymes with another line.

Brainstormed Rhyming Words

There once was a boy/girl named _____.

_____

_____

_____

_____

Brainstormed Rhyming Words

There once was a boy/girl from _____.

_____

_____

_____

_____

_____

_____

_____

4 Now invent your own first line and write a limerick to go with it!

_____

_____

_____

_____

_____

_____

_____

Teaching 10 Fabulous Forms of Poetry by Paul B. Janeczko
Scholastic Professional Books

Haiku

all night long
light shines in the eyes
of the carousel ponies

—*Penny Harter*

All summer long
the sixteen-story crane
bows and bows

—*J. Patrick Lewis*

November evening—
the wind from a passing truck
ripples a roadside puddle.

—*Cor van den Heuvel*

from the tar papered
tenement roof, pigeons
hot-foot into flight

—*Anita Wintz*

Teaching 10 Fabulous Forms of Poetry by Paul B. Janeczko   Scholastic Professional Books

Haiku

Stickball players shout
   as moonlight floods their field
      from curb to curb

              The sudden storm's dead…
                 petals from the dogwood tree
                   on the still pond

The young artist takes
   pains to paint a masterpiece:
      a smiling pumpkin

              The moaning snowplow
                shatters the frigid stillness
                 of a crystal night

Teaching 10 Fabulous Forms of Poetry by Paul B. Janeczko   Scholastic Professional Books

Haiku:

WORD-PAINTING IN 17 SYLLABLES

Nearly a thousand years ago in Japan, young poets frequently gathered at parties to write long collaborative poems called *renga*. After the poet with the best reputation wrote the first short section of the renga, his colleagues took turns writing other short parts. In the 15th century (see page 48), these short sections were released from the long poem and eventually developed into haiku. Although haiku have been popular in Japan for hundreds of years, they did not attract attention in Europe or America until the early part of this century.

In America, haiku captured the attention of poets like Amy Lowell, Ezra Pound, and William Carlos Williams. Part of a new breed of American poets, eager to alter traditional forms, they were drawn to haiku's precise images, its directness, and that it was free of the constraints of rhyme. The influence of haiku can be felt in the work of many 20th century poets. Today, there are a number of haiku journals attracting the work of hundreds of poets.

A haiku is a kind of verbal snapshot. Generally, a haiku will:

◎ contain 17 syllables in lines of 5, 7, and 5 syllables;
◎ include some sort of seasonal word or phrase, either directly (*winter wind*) or indirectly (*thunder crashed*); and some sensory image (*sight, sound, smell, touch*);
◎ focus on nature; and
◎ be written in the present tense about the present moment.

Writing Haiku

Students often feel haiku are easy poems to write because they are so short, yet it is precisely the 17-syllable limit that makes the form so challenging. Young writers must use their powers of observation as well as their sense of language to capture a scene in a very few words.

Looking at Haiku

REPRODUCIBLE #1 (page 42) asks students to read through the haiku on pages 38–39 several times, focusing on two of the main elements of the form: syllable count and the "seasonal" word or phrase. Before students do the syllable count, make sure they know that a syllable is a part of a word. You might refresh their memory by putting a few words on the board and asking students to count the syllables.

After counting the syllables in the haiku, students may notice that not every poem adheres to the 5-7-5 rule. This is a good time to remind them that while they should try their best to follow the rules of a haiku, they should not do so at the expense of the "spirit" of the poem. If a line has an extra syllable or a line is short a syllable, that's okay by me.

A key element of the haiku is the seasonal word or phrase. All of the sample haiku use indirect references to a season. In the second part of the "Looking at Haiku" worksheet, students look for these words or phrases. Review with students the first haiku, pointing out that *stickball* is a summer street game. If it had read *touch football players*, that would suggest autumn. After students have gone through all four haiku and written down their responses, share them out loud. Before handing out REPRODUCIBLE #2 ("Getting Ideas for Your Haiku"), take some time to brainstorm other words and phrases that suggest the various seasons. For example, *raking leaves* suggests autumn; *swimming in the sea* suggests summer.

Getting Ideas for Your Haiku

While most traditional Japanese haiku depict rural life, the city is full of moments that can be brought to life in haiku. The "frame" in REPRODUCIBLE #2 (pages 43–44) encourages students to focus on one aspect of the scene they select for their haiku. For instance, rather than writing about a snowy field, students might focus on a solitary child making a snowman there. Instead of depicting the street they live on, they could frame their poem around a bird pecking a crust of bread that someone has dropped on the sidewalk. Encourage students to list specific sensory details when they take notes about what they see in their frame: sight, sound, smell, taste, and touch. Haiku do not normally contain metaphors and similes. They're apt to be pure description—a snapshot in 17 syllables.

Drafting a Haiku

The third reproducible (page 45) for this section offers suggestions for drafting haiku. Help students by encouraging them to focus on the spirit and the intent first, and then attend to the poem's syllable count per line. Make sure they include a word or phrase that suggests a season and vivid, descriptive, "sense" words. Does the haiku "sound" like a snapshot? Remind them that any words that do not add to the vividness of the poem should be cut. And, as always, give your students the chance to read their poems aloud to a writing partner or to the class. Taking an audience into account often aids new writers in refining their work.

Students may ask if they should indent the second and third lines of their haiku. They can, if they wish, or all three lines can be flush left. English language haiku is printed a number of ways.

RESOURCES

To examine some other haiku formats, look for these anthologies:

Stone Bench in an Empty Park, edited by Paul B. Janeczko (Orchard, 2000), is a collection of urban haiku illustrated with black-and-white photos; *The Haiku Anthology*, edited by Cor van den Heuvel (Norton, 1999); and *Haiku Moment: An Anthology of Contemporary North American Haiku*, edited by Bruce Ross (Tuttle, 1993). *The Essential Haiku* (Ecco, 1994), edited by former Poet Laureate Robert Hass, examines the work of three Japanese haiku masters: Basho, Buson, and Issa.

Name _____ Date _____

Looking at Haiku

Before you begin to write your own haiku, look carefully at the examples of haiku on pages 38 and 39.

1 Read through the haiku a few times.

2 Now, read them again, aloud and more slowly this time. Count the syllables in each line. Mark each syllable with a small line, like this:

/ / / / /

The moaning snowplow

3 At the end of each line, write down the number of syllables in that line. Are there 17 syllables in each poem? Are there five syllables in each first line? Seven syllables in each middle line? Five syllables in each last line?

4 After you have made your syllable count, read them again. This time look for words that tell you which season each haiku describes. Underline the words that hint at a season, then write them on this chart:

Words	**Season**
#1 _____	_____
#2 _____	_____
#3 _____	_____
#4 _____	_____
#5 _____	_____
#6 _____	_____
#7 _____	_____
#8 _____	_____

Teaching 10 Fabulous Forms of Poetry by Paul B. Janeczko   Scholastic Professional Books

Name _____ Date _____

Getting Ideas for Your Haiku

Since a good haiku is written about a limited scene, it might help you to "frame" what you are looking at. Carefully cut out the frame provided on page 44. Take your frame with you to a spot that seems rich with images—the classroom window, the gym, or the block you live on. Hold up the frame in front of you at arm's length. Look only at what is inside the frame. If you notice something that might make a good haiku, write down a clear description on your note sheet, "Details To Capture" on page 44. For example, if you see birds fighting at the bird feeder, jot down some notes about that scene, including the sounds you hear (*scratching feet, beat of wings, screech of a blue jay*), the colors, and so forth. Don't concern yourself with anything that is outside your frame.

Teaching 10 Fabulous Forms of Poetry by Paul B. Janeczko   Scholastic Professional Books

Details to Capture
(Five Senses)

Sight: _____

_____

_____

Sound: _____

_____

_____

Touch: _____

_____

_____

Smell: _____

_____

_____

Taste: _____

_____

_____

Teaching 10 Fabulous Forms of Poetry by Paul B. Janeczko   Scholastic Professional Books

Cut along dotted line

Name _____ Date _____

Drafting Your Haiku

1 Look over your observations on the "Details To Capture" sheet (worksheet #2, page 44) and use these notes to describe—*in a single sentence*—a scene you saw. Remember that your haiku should be written in the present tense and be about the present moment. For example: *Flutter of wings as birds fight for the seeds at the bird feeder hanging in the oak tree.*

_____

_____

2 Once you have written your sentence, check to see if you've included some sensory images (sight, sound, smell, taste, and touch). Of course, you will not use all your senses in every poem, but it is the sense words that make the scene you are evoking come alive. You may wish to underline any sensory words in your sentence.

3 Check that you have included a hint to tell the reader which season is evoked in your haiku. Draw a circle around that seasonal word. If you don't have one, revise your sentence to include one.

4 Are there words in your draft that do not help create a clear image? Cross out these words. Remember, you are looking for the best, most vivid words when you write a poem.

5 Now that you have edited and pared down your sentence, write out the new version. My example from above might wind up being something like:

Flutter of wings birds fight for the seeds at the full bird feeder swinging in the oak.

Notice that I changed *hanging* to *swinging* in the last line. I thought it showed more action than *hanging*. Notice too that I kept the syllable count the same!

6 Next, write out your own sentence as a haiku, in three lines, like this:

> Flutter of wings
> birds fight for seeds at the full bird feeder
> swinging in the oak

7 Count the syllables. You will notice there are 4, 9, 5 syllables in the three lines. Practice tinkering with my syllables, especially in the middle line. Maybe we don't need *for seeds* because that's so obvious. If we cut out those words, we wind up with a 4, 7, 5 haiku, which is okay. Our revision now reads:

> Flutter of wings
> birds fight at the bird feeder
> swinging in the oak

8 Do you think these revisions improve the haiku? Why or Why not?

_____

9 Now that you have gone through the process of writing one haiku, use the space below to draft another one. Choose a different season, and perhaps create a different mood. For example, notice how poet Penny Harber creates a disquieting mood in her haiku. Instead of depicting a happy summer day of kids laughing on a carousel ride, she chooses night, and makes us feel pity for the inanimate ponies:

> all night long
> light shines in the eyes
> of the carousel ponies.

_____

_____

_____

Teaching 10 Fabulous Forms of Poetry by Paul B. Janeczko   Scholastic Professional Books

Senryu

A cloud of fat flies
hover near my locker…
old tuna sandwich

Filling the frosty dawn
my father's shouts and bellows:
car won't start…again

Grumpy bear growl
blends with chirp of rusty hinge:
Dad and Mom snoring

O, unlucky man
while eating shiny apple
you find half a worm

Senryu:

HAIKU WITH ATTITUDE

lthough there is some debate among haiku purists about what constitutes a senryu, I like to call it "haiku with attitude"—a poem written in the haiku form, but with wit and insight. The senryu (pronounced sener-you) focuses on human nature and events rather than on Nature itself. Consequently, the senryu most likely avoid the seasonal word or phrases common to haiku.

Like the haiku, the senryu originated as part of the *regna*, a long collaborative poem. The senryu were the inner sections of the regna recounting human events and actions. Toward the end of the 1600s, however, the senryu began to stand on its own. Senryu became a popular part of writing contests held in tea houses and wine shops. A "selector" would leave a group of "opening poems" (usually two or three lines long) for customers to complete with their own short poems. The selector would then collect the poems and publish the best in an anthology. To enter the competition, poets paid a small entry fee, and the money served both as prize money and as commission for the selector's work.

The senryu competitions had a kind of "can-you-top-this?" quality. Poets vied to see who could write the best poem to complete the opening lines. These writing competitions were most popular in the 1700s, when new contests were held almost every month. Most of the poets who entered were common laborers. Their poems had none of the polish and refinement of those written by upper-class haiku poets, such as Basho or Issa. By the middle of the 18th century, the senryu evolved from a short poem that completed another short poem into the three-line form we know today.

Writing Senryu

The senryu is a good poetic form to have your students write after they have written some haiku because it gives them an opportunity to further develop the observation skills used for haiku.

Observing People

Introduce your students to the senryu after they've had time to experiment with haiku. The senryu follows the haiku form and, like the haiku, requires careful observation. This time, however, students will observe human nature, rather than the natural world around them.

The first reproducible ("Observing People," page 50) for this section contains four note cards on which students jot down observations of people at several different locales. Before you give students their cards and turn them loose to observe, you might want to talk about some places that are good observation spots. Write some possible locations on the board as the students make suggestions: the mall, the library, the cafeteria, the playground, the supermarket, the park.

Now talk about the kinds of things students should be looking for, things that reveal human nature and events, things that they can have some fun with—but not make fun *of.* It's important to stress that the spirit of the senryu is not to mock individuals, but to capture a charming moment in their lives or a habit that is unique to them. For example, you might spy a moment of contradiction—your father eating an ice cream cone in his jogging suit. You might notice birds flying around the giant jets at the airport. Or the fast food worker who wears gloves and a hat to prepare food but doesn't cover his mouth when he coughs.

When students have completed the first worksheet (REPRODUCIBLE #1), they can begin drafting a senryu.

Brainstorming Pet Peeves

I've found that students easily discover topics for their senryu after brainstorming a list of their pet peeves. REPRODUCIBLE #2 (page 51) provides students with the space to list five such complaints. Try a "Complaint Swap," in which students can have some fun with a little "Can-You-Top-This?" As they discuss their peeves, students should take notes and add to their list. When they have finished brainstorming, they can work on a second senryu.

Completing a Senryu

The last line of a senryu is like the punch line of a joke. It often contains the unexpected. If you take a close look at the first two lines of the last senryu on page 47, you probably don't know why the man eating the shiny apple is unlucky. The third line tells us, and it's probably something we didn't expect. To help students get the hang of inventing humorous last lines, REPRODUCIBLE #3 (page 52) includes the two opening lines of four senryu. Ask students to come up with a good last line for each poem. Discuss their lines and have them do further work on the two senryu they drafted at the end of the "Observing People" and "Brainstorming Pet Peeves" reproducibles.

Some things to remind them of:

◎ The senryu is a poem, not simply a chance to complain or make fun of someone.

◎ Its form follows the 5-7-5 syllable count of a haiku, although it will probably not contain the seasonal word.

◎ A senryu also should have the sharply observed details found in a haiku.

◎ The last line needs to offer a funny flourish of some kind.

Name _____ Date _____

Observing People

Much of the best poetry comes from close observation of the world around us. A senryu will include "observational" humor about things found in *human* nature, so it's important to do some careful observing. Look for something that is out of whack, something that might reflect the way people think and act. Here is an observation I made at the airport:

Who ······ BIRD

Where ····· AIRPORT

What ····· FLYING AROUND THE HUGE JETS

After you have spent some time observing, fill out each of these observation note cards.

Who: _____

Where: _____

What: _____
_____

Who: _____

Where: _____

What: _____
_____

Who: _____

Where: _____

What: _____
_____

Who: _____

Where: _____

What: _____
_____

Use a separate sheet of paper to develop one of your observations into a senryu.

Teaching 10 Fabulous Forms of Poetry by Paul B. Janeczko

Scholastic Professional Books

Name _____ Date _____

Brainstorming Pet Peeves

Fill in these blanks with your pet peeves, those petty annoyances that make you want to scream! (Things like: People who talk during a movie, people who try to cut in line, a favorite TV show moved to a different night, noisy mosquitoes.)

1. _____

2. _____

3. _____

4. _____

5. _____

How can you turn one of your complaints into a senryu? Remember to be specific. For example, don't write about school lunch, describe a specific meal. Let's say you are writing about "sloppy joes." How can you have some fun with that? You might say something like:

> **Sloppy joes again...**
> **even the flies leave the cafe**
> **O, lucky flies!**

Use the space below to develop one of your pet peeves into a senryu.

_____

_____

_____

Name _____ Date _____

Completing a Senryu

H ere are the first two lines of several senryu. Think of a good closing line for each and write it in the space provided.

One warm summer night
I awake to rude music...

_____

Father snoring
At midnight, or can it be...

_____

Babysitter nags
She never goes anyplace...

_____

Snow falling at last
Down Deadman's Hill I race

_____

Teaching 10 Fabulous Forms of Poetry by Paul B. Janeczko   Scholastic Professional Books

Tanka

Early October
a sugar maple ablaze
at the end of the pond
its fire reflected
in the still water.

The chestnut vendor
must shout to be heard above
the October winds
his words rise, sail away
like the thin smoke from his stove.

Along the beach
footprints fill with the sea
fill with the sea
until they disappear
leaving only sand, only sea.

Lightning splits the sky
and for a moment we see
an empty playhouse
and just as suddenly
the back yard is black again.

Tanka:

🌱 5 Lines that Stir the Soul

At first glance, the tanka looks just like a haiku that is extended by two lines. But there is more to it than that. The tanka, from the Japanese word for "short poem," is a five-line poem that uses strong images to establish a mood. While literary devices like metaphor, simile, and personification are not used in haiku, they are often found in tanka. Because the English and Japanese languages are so different, there is little point in precisely counting syllables in an English tanka the way you would in Japanese. However, it is generally accepted that the tanka should have 31 syllables spread over five lines in this way: 5-7-5-7-7. Some tanka poets prefer to measure their lines in accented syllables: 2-3-2-3-3.

Whether you and your students count only accented syllables or all the syllables in a tanka, keep in mind that the spirit of the poem is far more important than blind adherence to syllable count. In fact, you will notice that the poems on page 53 contain a varying number of syllables. Because the tanka gives the poet greater opportunity for contemplation and reflection, as opposed to the strictly observational haiku, I recommend that you introduce the tanka to your class after practicing the haiku.

Writing Tanka

Since the tanka is related to the haiku in a number of ways, students who have written observational haiku can draw on that experience when working on their tankas. By writing the observational haiku, your students have had an opportunity to create a scene and, in some cases, establish a mood. Composing a tanka will allow them to work further on creating a mood in their poetry.

Feeling the Mood

Read the examples of tanka aloud to your students. Have them read each one silently and pay attention to how the mood of a piece of writing can be established with precise sensory words. Then hand out REPRODUCIBLE #1 ("Feeling the Mood," page 56), which asks students to pick out the sensory words in each poem and identify the mood evoked. If your students are not quite sure what a "mood" is, write some "mood words" on the board, like *quiet*, *tranquil, agitated, somber,* and discuss them. In one sense, a mood is how you feel when you read a poem, or the overall "feeling" of the scene.

The first poem, for example, draws mainly on the sense of sight: we see the tree ablaze, fire, the still water. Even though the autumn leaves of the sugar maple are ablaze with color, the mood of the poem is quiet. The second poem, on the other hand, appeals mostly to the sense of hearing, with its strong winds and vendor's shouts. Consequently, the mood of this poem is spirited and busy.

Drafting a Tanka

REPRODUCIBLE #2 (page 57) helps students to start taking notes that describe the scene they intend to write about in their tanka. Remind them to include sensory words. You might even ask them to be aware of the mood of the scene they are writing about. If students are not yet familiar with a thesaurus, this is a terrific moment to show them how this reference tool can help them find more vivid words for their writing.

After students have used their notes to write a draft (in class or at home), give them the time—and encouragement—to discuss their poems with their writing partners. Such dialogue is often quite productive.

Revising Your Tanka

Included in REPRODUCIBLE #3 (page 58) is a checklist of specific aspects of the tanka that writers should examine. Although writers need not create tanka that are perfect in syllable count, they should strive to come close. Remind students that the tanka is an observational poem, like the haiku, but the five-line format gives them some time to reflect on what they are describing. And as I've said before, it is more important to try to capture the spirit of this short poem.

As your students revise, be on the lookout for a poet who has made some worthwhile improvements on his or her first draft. With the poet's permission, you might write both versions on the board and let the class see how thoughtful revision can improve a piece of writing. You might also ask the poet to explain his/her revisions.

Name _____ Date _____

Feeling the Mood

As you read these tanka, underline the words and phrases that are connected to one of our senses: sight, sound, smell, taste and touch. After you have found the sensory words in the poem, describe the mood of the poem, or the feeling it creates, in the space provided.

Along the beach
footprints fill with the sea
fill with the sea
until they disappear
leaving only sand, only sea.

_____
_____
_____

Early October
a sugar maple ablaze
at the end of the pond
its fire reflected
in the still water.

_____
_____
_____

The chestnut vendor
must shout to be heard above
the October winds
his words rise, sail away
like the thin smoke from his stove.

_____
_____
_____

Lightning splits the sky
and for a moment we see
an empty playhouse
And just as suddenly
the back yard is black again.

_____
_____
_____

Name _____   Date _____

Drafting Your Tanka

A tanka doesn't need to have a seasonal setting. However, it's probably a good idea to include one in your first few poems, since this will help you actually *see* and *feel* the scene as you take notes. Here's a good way to get started:

1 Choose a scene you would like to write about.

2 Visit that scene in your imagination. Take some notes in the space below. Be alert to your senses as you jot down your ideas. Can you make any comparisons as you describe the scene? (For example: *the wind howls like a freight train, the sun is a gold coin, the snowflakes coasted to the ground.*)

3 After taking notes to capture the image and mood you want in your poem, circle the words you think will make that image come alive. Use these words when you begin drafting your tanka.

_____

_____

_____

_____

_____

_____

Teaching 10 Fabulous Forms of Poetry by Paul B. Janeczko   Scholastic Professional Books

Name _____ Date _____

Revising Your Tanka

Look carefully at your draft. You'll probably find places that need some tinkering. That's good because a draft *should* require some revising—otherwise it would be the final version, not a draft. To improve your tanka, consider the four points below. Check this list yourself and revise accordingly. Then, have a friend or writing partner read your tanka and write comments with these points in mind.

1 Does your poem come close to the syllable count of a tanka? Count the syllables and see if you come close. Remember not to be a slave to the guidelines, but use them to give your poem some structure.

Peer comments: _____

_____

2 Has your poem created the mood or feeling you were aiming for? Underline the parts you think do the job in your poem.

Peer comments: _____

_____

3 Has your poem created a strong image? Can you see the picture or hear it? Circle the sensory words in your tanka.

Peer comments: _____

_____

4 Have you used any figurative language or comparisons in your poem? Draw a box around any such words or phrases.

Peer comments: _____

_____

This checklist should help you capture some of the important elements of a good tanka.

Teaching 10 Fabulous Forms of Poetry by Paul B. Janeczko   Scholastic Professional Books

"Catcher Sings the Blues"

Crouching low, I sing the blues
The aches are now a part of me
Blocking home, I sing the blues
O, the aches are now a part of me
Bruises, bumps, and scrapes
Have worn me down, can't you see?

My knees sing the blues
They sing 'em when I stoop and bend
My knees sing the blues
O, they sing 'em when I stoop and bend
They crunch, crackle, pop
The hurtful noises never end.

My fingers sing the blues
When I grip a ball or make a fist
O, my fingers sing the blues
When I grip a ball or make a fist
The knuckles moan and cry
By fire every one is kissed.

Crouching low, I sing the blues
The aches are now a part of me
Blocking home, I sing the blues
O, these aches are now a part of me
Too many bruises, bumps, and scrapes
I'm nothing like I used to be.

No, nothing like I used to be.

Teaching 10 Fabulous Forms of Poetry by Paul B. Janeczko   Scholastic Professional Books

My Daddy

my daddy sings the blues
he plays it on his old guitar
my daddy sings the blues
and he plays it on an old guitar
he plucks it on the strings
and he sings about the way things are

he sings baby, baby, baby
I love you till the day I die
he sings baby, baby, baby
I love you till the day I die
well I hope you love me back
cause you know I don't want to cry

he sings 'Thaniel, 'Thaniel, 'Thaniel
boy I love you deed I do
he sings 'Thaniel, 'Thaniel, 'Thaniel,
boy I love you deed I do
well you're a mighty fine fella
and son I'm so proud of you

my daddy sings the blues
he plays it on his old guitar
yeah my daddy sings the blues
and he plays it on that old guitar
he ain't never been on TV
but to me he's a great big star

—*Eloise Greenfield*

Teaching 10 Fabulous Forms of Poetry by Paul B. Janeczko   Scholastic Professional Books

Blues Poems:
LETTING THE SPIRIT SING

Although its roots can be found in Africa, the blues have been a rich part of the American music scene for some 150 years. The blues grew from the oral tradition of southern slaves in 19th-century America, who sang work songs in the fields. These songs often took the form of "field hollers," a kind of singing talk among the slaves. While the majority of blues songs were about the death, loss, and frustrations of a slave's wretched life, they frequently contained hope that the human spirit would triumph over such hardships.

The traditional blues stanza has three lines. All three lines rhyme; the second being a slight variation of the first line. Langston Hughes wrote a number of blues poems in which he sometimes broke the three long lines into six shorter lines. "Catcher Sings the Blues" follows this variation, with three or four stressed syllables per line. If you listen to some of the blues masters—like Robert Johnson, Bessie Smith, and Sonny Boy Williamson—it won't take long before you find yourself caught up in the rhythm of the blues.

It simply can't be emphasized enough, however, that the essential part of a blues poem is the *spirit*. The poem recounts life's miseries, from the serious (having no money) to the less so (having too much homework).

Writing A Blues Poem

Since the blues poem deals with personal and world issues, it provides students with an excellent opportunity to give voice to some of their important concerns. It gives you the chance to see what's really on the minds of your students.

Feeling the Blues

It is crucial that students understand the spirit of the blues before they begin writing a blues poem. I mentioned some blues singers whose work would certainly go a long way toward filling the room with the blues. In addition to music, I would suggest you share some blues poems with your students. Although many blues poems are inappropriate for children, you can read Langston Hughes' "Evenin' Air Blues" and "Po' Boy Blues" with them. You can also use two poems by Eloise Greenfield: "My Daddy" (on page 60) and "Watching the World Go By."

Learning the Blues Form

After students have had a chance to hear some blues songs and poems, look carefully at REPRODUCIBLE #1 (page 63), and the example, "Catcher Sings the

Blues" on page 59. REPRODUCIBLE #2 (page 65) features questions intended to help students recognize some of the patterns in a blues poem. They should notice that:

◎ lines 1 and 3 of a blues stanza are repeated (with slight variation).

◎ lines 2 and 4 are repeated (with slight variation).

◎ line 6 rhymes with line 4 (and ends with the same word as line 2).

◎ line 5 is the only line in the blues stanza that has no rhyme.

At first, it might seem complicated, but encourage students to see that the six-line stanza really has only four lines, since two are repeated.

Thinking About the Blues

After reading a few blues poems and listening to some blues singers, use REPRODUCIBLE #2 (pages 65–66) to help your students choose subjects or themes for their poems. This exercise allows students to explore two different types of topics, "World Issues" and "Personal Issues."

Once they have written down some ideas and selected a topic for their first blues poem, students should use the second part of REPRODUCIBLE #2 ("Looking for Details") to identify specific reasons why that topic gives them the blues. They cannot write "I Got the Little Brother Blues" unless they can show the reader why or how that sibling gives them the blues. The more specific their complaints, the truer the poem will sound. They will need enough detail to write a three- or four-stanza blues poem.

Writing a Blues Poem

Before students begin working on their poems, suggest a few ways they might begin drafting.

◎ Write about someone else who has the blues, perhaps the principal or a teenage sister. Such a poem might begin with a line like, "My big sister's got the blues," and go on to show why that person has the blues.

◎ In the opening line, identify the person or thing that gives them the blues. A poem that begins with "I got the babysitter blues" would go on to detail the reasons why a babysitter gives him/her the blues.

◎ You may also use my poem, "Catcher Sings the Blues" (page 59) as a model. Although the blues are traditionally about serious issues, your students can easily include exaggeration in their poems to add a tongue-in-cheek quality.

Editing Your Blues Poem

Since the blues poem is from the oral tradition, it is important that your students read their poems aloud to a writing partner as they revise. Remind the listeners to focus of the sound and spirit of the poem and to try their best to suggest spots that need some work. Some finger snapping and foot tapping might help!

Name _____ Date _____

Learning the Blues Form

As you read "Catcher Sings the Blues," here are some things to do:

1 Underline the lines in each stanza that are repeated and draw a connecting line between them. If you have colored markers or pencils, you can use the same color to show the lines that are repeated.

2 Circle the end words that have the same sound and draw a line between these words.

3 Draw a box around a specific detail or two in each stanza.

4 Mark the stressed syllables in each line.

Teaching 10 Fabulous Forms of Poetry by Paul B. Janeczko   Scholastic Professional Books

Name _____ Date _____

"My Daddy"

This poem by Eloise Greenfield is a little different from most blues poems because it doesn't sing of someone's misery. Rather, it tells about a young boy's love for his father. Read the poem again, then try these activities:

1 Find three lines that show how the dad feels about his son.

_____

_____

_____

2 Check the rhyme scheme of this poem. Does it follow the pattern of a blues poem?

_____

_____

_____

3 If you were going to write a blues poem about someone you love, what would you say about them? Write some ideas below:

_____

_____

_____

4 Later you will write a traditional blues poem. After you have completed it, try to write one stanza of a blues poem like "My Daddy," in which you write about someone you love.

Teaching 10 Fabulous Forms of Poetry by Paul B. Janeczko   Scholastic Professional Books

Name _____ Date _____

Thinking About the Blues

W hat gives you the blues? What makes you sad? What depresses you? What frustrates you? What are your pet peeves? It could be a large issue that you see in the world around you, like violence or prejudice, or it might be a more personal issue, something like a broken heart, the loss of a loved one, or dealing with divorce. Of course, there are plenty of smaller personal issues that can give you the blues, like too much homework or a smelly locker room.

So, what gives you the blues? Think about it, then write down your ideas in the columns below. When you've completed your lists, circle the two topics that you think would work best for you. Pick one from each list.

World Issues	**Personal Issues**
_____	_____
_____	_____
_____	_____
_____	_____
_____	_____
_____	_____
_____	_____
_____	_____

Name _____ Date _____

Thinking About the Blues, Part 2:
Looking for Details

1 There are specific things in "Catcher Sings the Blues" on page 59 that give the narrator the blues. What are they? Read the poem again and underline them.

2 Now, choose a topic of your own that you think will make a good blues poem. Write it in the space below, then list specific details about the topic that make you blue. Try to come up with at least six details because your poem will include three or four stanzas. For example, if you are going to write about how your little sister gives you the blues, your details might include things like:

◎ whines at bedtime

◎ always asks for a piece of my candy

◎ tells my parents when I do something I'm not supposed to do

◎ listens in on my phone conversations

◎ goes in my room when I'm not home

Your Topic: _____

Your Details:

1. _____

2. _____

3. _____

4. _____

5. _____

Teaching 10 Fabulous Forms of Poetry by Paul B. Janeczko   Scholastic Professional Books

Name _____ Date _____

Editing Your Blues Poem

Write the draft of your blues poem on a separate sheet of paper. Edit your poem by reviewing these elements of the blues poem.

◎ Rhyme

Circle the rhyming word at the end of each line and draw a line connecting it to the other words it rhymes with.

◎ Rhythm

Read your poem aloud. Each line should have three or four beats. Make a mark above each syllable you stress as you read your poem. If you have a writing partner, read your poems aloud to each other. As you do, listen for the blues beat in the poem. If it's not strong, take a closer look at your poem and see what you can do to get that beat.

◎ Details

Read your poem to yourself and underline each detail that you find. With each detail, ask yourself if you can tell which of your senses— sight, sound, smell, taste, or touch—that detail appeals to.

◎ Spirit

Since the spirit of a blues poem is so important, ask a writing partner to read your poem aloud to you. Close your eyes. Listen for the music in your words. Can you snap your fingers to the beats in each line? Can you feel the misery in the poem, even if it's exaggerated? Do you think someone else who hears your poem will hear what you hear?

The Wreck of the Hesperus

'T WAS the schooner Hesperus,
    That sailed the wintry sea;
And the skipper had taken his little daughter,
    To bear him company.

Blue were her eyes as the fairy-flax,
    Her cheeks like the dawn of day,
And her bosom white as the hawthorn buds
    That ope in the month of May.

The skipper he stood beside the helm,
    His pipe was in his mouth,
And he watched how the veering flaw did blow
    The smoke now West, now South.

Then up and spake an old Sailor,
    Had sailed the Spanish Main,
"I pray thee, put into yonder port,
    For I fear a hurricane.

"Last night the moon had a golden ring,
    And to-night no moon we see!"
The skipper he blew a whiff from his pipe,
    And a scornful laugh laughed he.

Teaching 10 Fabulous Forms of Poetry by Paul B. Janeczko   Scholastic Professional Books

Colder and colder blew the wind,
    A gale from the North-east;
The snow fell hissing on the brine,
    And the billows frothed like yeast.

Down came the storm, and smote amain
    The vessel in its strength;
She shuddered and paused, like a frightened steed,
    Then leaped her cable's length.

"Come hither! come hither! my little daughter,
    And do not tremble so;
For I can weather the roughest gale
    That ever wind did blow."

He wrapped her warm in his seaman's coat
    Against the stinging blast;
He cut a rope from broken spar,
    And bound her to the mast.

"O father! I hear the church-bells ring,
    O say, what may it be?
" 'T is a fog-bell on a rock-bound coast!"
    And he steered for the open sea.

"O father! I hear the sound of guns,
    O say, what may it be?"
"Some ship in distress, that cannot live
    In such angry sea!"

"O father! I see a gleaming light,
  O say, what may it be?"
But the father answered never a word,
  A frozen corpse was he.

Lashed to the helm, all stiff and stark,
  With his face turned to the skies,
The lantern gleamed through the gleaming snow
  On his fixed and glassy eyes.

Then the maiden clasped her hands and prayed,
  That saved she might be;
And she thought of Christ, who stilled the wave,
  On the Lake of Galilee.

And fast through the midnight dark and drear,
  Through the whistling sleet and snow,
Like a sheeted ghost, the vessel swept
  Towards the reef of Norman's Woe.

And ever the fitful gusts between
  A sound came from the land;
It was the sound of the trampling surf,
  On the rocks and the hard sea-sand.

The breakers were right beneath her bows,
  She drifted a dreary wreck,
And a whooping billow swept the crew
  Like icicles from her deck.

Teaching 10 Fabulous Forms of Poetry by Paul B. Janeczko   Scholastic Professional Books

She struck where the white and fleecy waves
    Looked soft as carded wool.
But the cruel rocks, they gored her side
    Like the horns of an angry bull.

Her rattling shrouds, all sheathed in ice,
    With the masts went by the board;
Like a vessel of glass, she stove and sank,
    Ho! ho! The breakers roared!

At daybreak, on the bleak sea-beach,
    A fisherman stood aghast,
To see the form of a maiden fair,
    Lashed to a drifting mast.

The salt sea was frozen on her breast,
    The salt tears in her eyes;
And he saw her hair, like the brown sea-weed,
    On the billows fall and rise.

Such was the wreck of the Hesperus,
    In the midnight and the snow!
Christ save us all from a death like this
    On the reef of Norman's Woe!

—*Henry Wadsworth Longfellow*

Teaching 10 Fabulous Forms of Poetry by Paul B. Janeczko   Scholastic Professional Books

The Ballad:

STORYTELLING IN VERSE

L ike the blues poem, the ballad has its origin in song. Wandering minstrels sang tales of love and death, heroes and heroines, long before they were ever collected and written down. This oral tradition of passing on of ballads is similar, in some ways, to the way we sometimes hear a song on the radio and memorize it, without ever seeing the words in print.

As peoples emigrated, they took their songs with them. So it was that the British and Scottish ballads of the 15th and 16th centuries found their way to this country. And, as our nation grew, so did the oral tradition of ballads. Pioneers brought their European ballads West, and new ballads arose to chronicle the pioneer experience. Looking through the folk literature of this country, you can find ballads about our heroes and heroines, the settling of the American West, and the exploits of Yukon adventurers. In many countries, the ballad was one of the first forms of literature.

Because the ballad is based on an oral tradition, it is difficult to come up with a specific set of rules that fit them all. However, there are a few things most ballads have in common. They are usually written in four-line stanzas, or quatrains. The lines generally feature three or four iambic feet (an unstressed syllable followed by a stressed syllable). The second and the fourth line of each stanza rhyme. Sometimes the final line is repeated, making a five-line stanza. A ballad will frequently close with a summary stanza.

In addition to the elements above, there are other aspects of the ballad that give it its character. Ballads are narrative-driven, with little attention paid to character development. Action is developed through dialogue, and the language is simple and direct. Ballads often tell of ghosts and supernatural phenomena, love and death, unrequited love and lovers avenged. They also tell of larger-than-life bandits and outlaws, heroes and villains. Other famous examples include the likes of Jesse James, Sam Bass, Tom Dooley, and Casey Jones.

Writing a Ballad

Some students take to ballad writing like ducks to water, relishing a form that gives them more room to spin a yarn, to rhyme, and write many stanzas. Other students may be daunted by the notion of telling a story in verse. Regardless, it's a good form for students to try—and a good one to use in social studies, when you want to offer students a creative way to show what they've learned about a figure or event in history.

Looking at the Poem

Before trying their own, students should take a close look at "The Wreck of the Hesperus" to learn what makes a good ballad. The first step is to read the ballad out loud. This can be done in small groups, as individuals, or as a read-around. Ask volunteers to read aloud the entire poem. Or ask several students to read different parts of the poem. One might function as the narrator, while others can read the parts spoken by the characters: the daughter, the father, and the old sailor. Remind students to listen for:

◎ The plot of the ballad. What happens to whom in the poem?

◎ The rhythm and rhyme. Can they hear which words rhyme? Can they hear the repetition?

After students have heard the poem, use REPRODUCIBLE #1, which asks them to write down some of the things they noticed in the ballad. It also asks them to try to come up with an alternative ending to the poem. This new ending, a stanza of four or five lines, is a preliminary step to having them to write a ballad with a writing partner.

Brainstorming with a Partner

Because the ballad is usually a long poem, I suggest allowing students to work with a partner on this project. REPRODUCIBLE #2 takes students through two steps in the ballad-writing process: finding a subject—either a person or an event—and writing a brief prose story that can be transformed into a poem.

Before students begin working on this reproducible, discuss how to choose a topic. If students want to focus on a person as the subject of their ballad, remind them that the person they choose must have some heroic quality about him/her that can be recounted in the ballad. Sports figures are good possibilities, Michael Jordan or Mark McGwire. Other possibilities include an astronaut like Sally Ride, an Arctic explorer like Matthew Henson, and an activist like Jacques Cousteau. However, ballads can also be about ordinary people who do extraordinary things.

In addition to "The Wreck of the Hesperus," share other ballads with your students, so they can see the qualities and characteristics of this folk tradition. Longfellow wrote a number of ballads. You can also try "Danny Deever" and "Gunga Din," by Rudyard Kipling, "The Cremation of Sam McGee," "The Shooting of Dan McGrew," by Robert W. Service, and "The Rime of the Ancient Mariner," by Samuel Taylor Coleridge. Look at *Folk Song U.S.A.* by John A. and Alan Lomax, and *The Ballad of America* by John Anthony Scott.

As far as historical events are concerned, suggest something tragic like the sinking of the *Titanic* or the explosion aboard the *Challenger*. Choosing a historical event is a good opportunity for students to gather research for their poem. Since the ballad is plot-oriented, students need to know the basic facts surrounding the event. The ballad-based-on-historical-event is also a good chance for students to explore local history or maybe even family history.

Students need not write about a real character in a historical situation. They might, for example, write a ballad about a heroic girl on board the *Titanic*, or about a historical or sports figure in a fictional setting, something like Mark McGwire leaving his sick bed to hit a dramatic home run to win the World Series.

Plotting The Ballad

Before handing out REPRODUCIBLE #3, reread "The Wreck of the Hesperus" and outline the conflict and the main events of that story in a way that allows your students to see the narrative progression in the story. REPRODUCIBLE #3 guides them through the important ingredients of their ballad: main character, supporting characters, main conflict, its resolution, and the steps leading to that resolution. Remind students that the ballad is a good, old-fashioned story—maybe a little sentimental, maybe a little melodramatic—action packed as it moves toward its conclusion.

Name _____   Date _____

Exploring the Ballad

Read "The Wreck of the Hesperus" again and do the following:

1 Circle the words that rhyme and draw a line connecting the rhyming words.

2 Mark off the stressed syllables in the first five stanzas of the poem. What pattern for the stressed syllables do you notice in these stanzas?

_____

_____

3 Think of a different ending for this ballad, perhaps one that is happier, or, one that might surprise the reader. In the space below, summarize your new ending in a few sentences:

_____

_____

_____

_____

_____

_____

4 On another sheet of paper, take your idea for a new ending and write it as four-line stanzas to end the poem.

Teaching 10 Fabulous Forms of Poetry by Paul B. Janeczko   Scholastic Professional Books

Name _____ Date _____

Brainstorming with a Partner

With a writing partner, jot down some ideas for your ballad in the spaces below.

1 Name three people you admire a great deal, or three people who have done something heroic.

Who Are They?   **What Have They Done?**

◎ _____

◎ _____

◎ _____

2 List below three spectacular events from history. Then, on the back of this sheet, briefly answer the journalist's basic questions about each event: Who? What? When? Where? How? and Why?

◎ _____

◎ _____

◎ _____

Teaching 10 Fabulous Forms of Poetry by Paul B. Janeczko   Scholastic Professional Books

3 Choose a person or an event from your list and write a brief story about that subject. Your story can be simple but exciting, or sad, or romantic. Give your story a happy ending if you want to.

_____

_____

_____

_____

_____

_____

_____

_____

_____

_____

_____

_____

_____

_____

Name _____ Date _____

Planning Your Ballad

Before you begin writing your ballad, make sure you know the following part of the poem:

1 Who is the main character? _____

2 Who are the supporting characters? _____
_____

3 What is the main conflict in the story? _____
_____
_____
_____

4 How is the conflict resolved at the end of the ballad? _____
_____
_____
_____

5 Name four or five important steps in the plot of your ballad.

◎ _____

◎ _____

◎ _____

◎ _____

◎ _____

Teaching 10 Fabulous Forms of Poetry by Paul B. Janeczko   Scholastic Professional Books

```
          A
       GIRAFFE
          I
          S
          S
          O
          T
          A
          L
          L
            A
            N
            D
       HIS HEAD IS SO
     FAR ABOVE HIS LEGS
      HE PROBABLY CAN'T SEE
          H     T     E     K
          I     O     L     N
          S     E     S     E
                S     E     E
          A           B     S
          D     O     E
          O     R     L     A
          R           O     N
          A     A     W     D
          B     N
          L     Y     H     E
          E     T     I     L
                H     S     B
                I           O
                N           W
                G           S❖    —Maureen W. Armour
```

STOWAWAY —*Robert Carola*

O, Christmas Tree!

```
                  A
                 ng
                e l r
               e d b l
              uedud
             drumyel
            lowhook
           tinselblue
         popcornpopcorn
          flickergreen
         birdbluetinsel
        redgarlandredgar
        redlocomotivebear
       mousegreenredblue
      tinselpuppygreenblue
    popcornpopcornpopcornpopcorn
     flickerredducktinselred
    canbluekittenorangegreen
   garlandredgarlandredgarland
   tinselbluetrumpetbluedudblue
   yellowelfSantagreentinselred
  popcornpopcornpopcornpopcornpopcornpopcor
   bluepuppyMrs.Clausredbluetinsel
 Donneryellowblinkcandycandycaneorange
 redgarlandredgarlandredgarlandredga
 yellowgreenhooktinselflickerredblue
 cabooseredblueBlitzenPranceryellowblue
 popcornpopcornpopcornpopcornpopcornpopcornpopcornpopc
  tinselredblinksledyelloworangedudRudolph
 elfNativityballyellowgreentinselcandycane
 greendudDrummerBoybluepuppywithslippergreen
 redgarlandredgarlandredgarlandredgarlandredga
 Dancerredbluetinselgnomecandycanegreencardinal
popcornpopcornpopcornpopcornpopcornpoprcornpopcornpopcornpopcornpop
tinselRonaldMcDonaldredflickeryellowbluetinselblue
```

ST
AND

Teaching 10 Fabulous Forms of Poetry by Paul B. Janeczko   Scholastic Professional Books

Concrete Poems:

WHEN WORDS TAKE SHAPE

The term "concrete poetry" was coined in the 1950s in Europe, but the idea of a "shape poem" has been around for a long time. Although it is uncertain when shape or pattern poems first appeared in Western literature, there are some surviving examples in classical Latin dating back to the fourth century. Later, British metaphysical poet George Herbert wrote shape poems in the early 1600s, and in 1865, Lewis Carroll created a visual poem about a mouse tail in *Alice's Adventures in Wonderland*. Concrete poetry reached its peak more recently in the 1960s and 1970s in the United States and Europe. And although it has never been as popular as it was during those years, a number of poets continue to write concrete poems.

This may be the first time you have taken a close look at concrete poems, so let me point out a few things you can expect from them. Because of the way a concrete poem utilizes letters, type size, and space, you cannot read it in the same way you read a conventional poem. In some cases, it cannot be read aloud. However, you can look at a concrete poem the way you look at a painting. A good concrete poem will catch your eye with interesting fonts, colors or symbols, or by the way the words are arranged on the page. Words are used visually for more dramatic effect. A concrete poem utilizes the space of the page and the shape of the letters and words in ways that conventional poetry does not. At times, a concrete poem may simply seem like a collage of words and letters, but it actually uses this arrangement of letters and space to emphasize the meaning of the poem.

Writing A Concrete Poem

A concrete poem can be written in a number of ways. I've included examples on pages 79–80. The simplest concrete poem modifies a single word to illustrate the meaning of that word, as Robert Carola does with "Stowaway." Other concrete poems make pictures by varying the lengths of the lines to create the shape of an object, as Maureen W. Armour does with "A Giraffe," and as I do in "O, Christmas Tree!" Of course, there are endless variations on these possibilities.

Distribute copies of the examples on pages 79–80 and ask students whether they think these are poems. In my experience, some students will answer with a resounding "yes," and be intrigued by this new way to play with language. Others may feel that these are not really poems because they don't rhyme or tell a story. This is an excellent chance to discuss the notion that while poetry comes in many different forms, *all poetry involves an inventive use of language*. Concrete poetry is another way to write a poem.

RESOURCES

Four books of concrete poems that are worth looking for are:

Robert Froman. *Seeing Things.* Thomas Y. Crowell, 1974.

Joan Bransfield Graham. *Splish Splash.* Ticknor & Fields, 1994.

Paul B. Janeczko, ed. *A Poke In the I.* Candlewick Press, 2001.

J. Patrick Lewis. *Doodle Dandies: Poems That Take Shape.* Atheneum, 1999.

Also study Guillaume Apollinaire, a French poet who wrote in the late 1800s and was killed in World War I. He is one of the most successful practitioners of concrete poems, which he called *calligrammes.*

Writing a Single-Word Concrete Poem

REPRODUCIBLE #1 (page 83) invites students to examine the word *explode* and think of ways to make that word more interesting. Give students five or ten minutes to brainstorm some possibilities on their own. Then let them discuss their ideas with a partner. By then, the room should be about to "explode" with great ideas. Ask students to share their ideas and demonstrate them on the board or on chart paper.

The second part of this exercise asks students to list some words which, like *explode*, have the potential to be turned into a single-word concrete poem. Ask students to think of words and phrases that are visual or involve action: *soar, enlarge, sink.* An observational stroll around the school or neighborhood might give kids a chance to notice—and take notes. When students have come up with a short list of possible words, they can select the single word that they think would work best and write their poem at the bottom of the worksheet (or on another sheet of paper).

Exploring a Shape Concrete Poem

REPRODUCIBLE #2 (pages 84–85) helps young writers to try another variation of a concrete poem: a shape poem. Students begin by listing some objects with distinct shapes—like truck, snake, butterfly, bridge—then choose the object that they most want to write about and sketch it on the page. Next, students are asked to think more carefully about the shape and list some of its specific qualities, the things it does or that are done with it. For example, someone might write about a baseball: *round, smooth, white with red stitches, grass-stained, flies through the air, people throw it, hit it, chase it, and get autographs on it.*

Since the best poems, whether concrete or "conventional," are built with specific details, students need to think of associations the object conjures for them. A baseball might remind them of a game they watched with a friend, or one in which they made (or missed) a game-ending catch. These sorts of telling details should find their way into the poem.

Drafting Your Shape Poem

At this point, your students should have selected a shape and compiled a list of descriptive details they want to include in their poems. REPRODUCIBLE #3 ("Drafting Your Shape Concrete Poem") gives guidance as they draft their poems. It also provides them with a brief checklist to think about as they work. You might suggest that students and partners use the checklist to question each other about their poems. Sometimes a fresh perspective from a trusted peer can be helpful.

Name _____ Date _____

Writing a Single-Word Concrete Poem

1 What can you do with the word **EXPLODE** to make it look more interesting on the page? As you work on your "explode" poem in the space below, consider changing the size of the letters and utilizing space and color.

2 Make a list of other words that might make an exciting single-word concrete poem. Try to think of dramatic things in nature, like *lightning*, or everyday things, like *electricity*. Any words that suggest action work well, such as *climb, rodeo, curdle, bridge, waterfall.*

1. _____

2. _____

3. _____

4. _____

5. _____

3 Take one of these words and turn it into a concrete poem on the back of this page.

Teaching 10 Fabulous Forms of Poetry by Paul B. Janeczko   Scholastic Professional Books

Name _____ Date _____

Exploring a Shape Concrete Poem

1 Make a list of objects that have simple or distinctive shapes, like a baseball or an umbrella.

1. _____   4. _____

2. _____   5. _____

3. _____   6. _____

2 Pick the object that appeals to you the most and sketch that shape below.

Teaching 10 Fabulous Forms of Poetry by Paul B. Janeczko   Scholastic Professional Books

3 What can you say about this shape? Can you think of specific qualities the object has? Write them here:

_____

_____

_____

4 What are some things that it does or that are done with it? Write them here:

_____

_____

_____

5 Think of a few things you associate with the object. For example, a baseball might make you think of a game you saw with a friend, the ball park, hot dogs, an ace pitcher. Write your ideas here:

_____

_____

_____

_____

_____

_____

Name _____ Date _____

Drafting Your Shape Concrete Poem

1 Reread the notes you've written on worksheet #2. Without thinking about it too much, quickly circle the words and ideas you like best. Read them aloud to yourself. It will probably sound like a poem in the making!

2 Next, with a pencil, lightly outline the object (make it as big as possible) on a separate piece of paper. This is the basic shape of your poem. Start writing words along the outline of the object. Think of words that describe the subject or are related to it. For example, if you are writing a poem about a rainstorm, you might use words like—*puddles, wet feet, downpour*—written at an angle to imitate driving rain.

3 Now that you have a rough draft of your shape poem, you're ready to refine it. Your concrete poem is almost like a painting, so you want to make sure that it catches the reader's eye. As you work on your revision, give some thought to:

◎ **The size and style of the type**

Do you want to hand write your poem? Use a computer to set your words in tiny type or huge type? Use bold, italics, or a fancy font?

◎ **The color and shape of the letters**

Would your poem stand out with colorful letters? With uniquely shaped letters? Try cutting letters out of magazines to make the words you want to include.

◎ **The space in and around the shape**

Should your poem be centered in the page with a lot of "white space" around it? Should the shape be large or small?

4 Looking at your rough draft for reference, create another sketch of your shape poem, then do a final version on another sheet of paper.

Teaching 10 Fabulous Forms of Poetry by Paul B. Janeczko   Scholastic Professional Books

In such a day, in September or October, Walden is a perfect forest mirror, set round with stones as precious to my eye as if fewer or rarer. Nothing so fair, so pure, at the same time so large, as a lake, perchance, lies on the surface of the earth. Sky water. It needs no fence. Nations come and go without defiling it. It is a mirror which no stone can crack, whose quicksilver will never wear off, whose gilding Nature continually repairs; no storms; no dust, can dim its surface ever fresh; —a mirror in which all impurity presented to it sinks, swept and dusted by the sun's hazy brush....

—*from "The Ponds" by Henry David Thoreau*

Teaching 10 Fabulous Forms of Poetry by Paul B. Janeczko   Scholastic Professional Books

Walden Pond

Walden is a perfect forest mirror:
so fair
so pure
so large
Set round with stones
Sky water
needs no fence.
A mirror
no stone can crack.
Quicksilver
will never wear off.
No storms.
no dust.
ever fresh.
A mirror.

Teaching 10 Fabulous Forms of Poetry by Paul B. Janeczko   Scholastic Professional Books

Found Poems:
EDITING AT ITS EXTREME

There are people who will tell you that found poetry is not really poetry at all. These are the same people who might tell you that concrete poetry isn't really poetry either. Listen politely to such nay-sayers, but recognize that they more than likely have a traditional view of poetry that doesn't allow for much "out of the box" word play. As you will see, students get a kick out of "writing" found poetry.

What exactly is a "found" poem? A found poem is culled from the language of a piece of writing that was not written as verse, such as an essay, a letter, or a newspaper article. The reader discovers the poetic elements of the prose. In a true found poem, none of the words are changed, and the sequence of the words is likewise unaltered. Poet and writer Annie Dillard comments that found poetry is "editing at its extreme: writing without composing."

One of the important things about writing found poetry is that it encourages kids to be aware of the language around us, to see how language not intended as poetry can have poetic qualities and evoke a strong emotional response from a reader. Another benefit of writing found poetry is that it can get young writers out of the "rhyming rut," because it focuses, instead, on the significance of individual words to a poem as a whole.

Writing a Found Poem

Before your class does any writing, you will need stacks of magazines and newspapers (wedding announcements and obituaries are often rich sections to explore), novels and nonfiction books, clothing catalogs—even restaurant menus! These are the sources from which the found poems will spring, so the more varied and extensive your supply, the better. A few weeks before you introduce found poetry, ask students to start bringing in material. (Leftover material will provide pictures for posters and collages to go with student poems.)

Because this form will be new to most of your students, you should expect a little uncertainty from them. Maybe even a little chaos—that good, creative chaos—as they paw through magazines and catalogs to find the right words for their found poems. Your students will feel the excitement of trying something new.

Looking at a Found Poem

Begin by giving your students a copy of the excerpt from *Walden Pond* (page 87). Ask them to read through it once, then go back and underline all the descriptive and poetic words and phrases. Discuss the choices they make. Next, hand out a copy of my found poem, "Walden Pond" (page 88). Let them read through it and see the choices I made. I suspect that some students may have made many of the same choices in their underlining activity. Remember, however, the point is not to check to see how many kids picked the same words I did. Rather, it is to urge the kids to look at and listen carefully to language.

After this exercise, students should be ready to try a found a poem of their own. The first step is for them to find a suitable article. (I use the word "article" for simplicity's sake; any piece of prose writing will do.) This may take too much time for one class, so you might give students a few days to select an article at home. Another way to get this poetry unit started, especially if your class needs a more directed approach, is simply to give students five or six pre-selected prose pieces to choose from.

Looking for Poetic Language

Once all of your students have selected an article, you can give them REPRODUCIBLE #1 ("Looking for Poetic Language," page 92). This worksheet asks them to read the article carefully and underline the poetic words they find, "words that surprise or astound" them. The last section of the reproducible asks students to jot down a few of their selections and then explain how or why a word or phrase captured their attention. Was it an image the word conjures for them? Does it remind them of something? Or do they just like the sound of the word?

Drafting a Found Poem

REPRODUCIBLE #2 (page 93) takes students to the next level in the found poetry writing process. The exercise instructs students to write each of their words on an index card or a small piece of paper. Does rearranging the words give them new ideas for their poem? While some purists will argue that such juggling of the sequence of the words is not permitted in a true found poem, I think it's perfectly acceptable. By playing with words, young writers begin to understand the importance of word choice (diction) and word order (syntax) in writing a poem. By omitting words, they also learn the importance of economy in good poetry.

Working on Line Breaks

After students have written a draft, they can use the third reproducible, "Working on Line Breaks," (page 94) to experiment with line breaks and understand how the arrangement of words on a page can also affect a poem. In free verse poetry, line breaks are often confusing to young writers. There are no set rules about which words belong on a line. However, young writers need to remember that the words they put on a line must make sense together, whether it is two words or a complete sentence of many words. The words on a line needn't offer the complete thought of a sentence, but they have to "belong" together. This is often a tough concept for young writers to grasp, but the more free verse they read and write, the deeper their understanding of line breaks will be.

Another way for students to write found poems is to leaf through magazines and newspapers, clipping words and phrases from headlines. They can use these words to make something of a collage-like poem. With this type of poem, young writers can see the effects that different print fonts, colors, and sizes have on their poems. This works well as a homework assignment to be completed over a few days. I also suggest you limit the number of words they can use for their poem. Fifty is a nice round (and manageable) number. As students work on their headline poems, remind them that the purpose of the activity is to look for words that connect to one another, words that surprise and delight, not to see how many different headlines they can cram into a found poem.

R E S O U R C E S

Annie Dillard's book, *Mornings Like This: Found Poems* (HarperCollins, 1995), is a collection of found poems from various sources. It includes an informative introduction to the form and the poet's process.

Stephen Dunning, M. Joe Eaton and Malcolm Glass wrote *For Poets* (Scholastic, 1975), for the long-gone Scholastic Literature Unit. This book includes a number of found poetry activities.

Name _____ Date _____

Looking for Poetic Language

1 Find an article that strikes you as a good source for a found poem. It should be something that you enjoy reading. Read it very carefully, several times, looking for words or phrases that catch your eye.

2 As you read through the article, underline all the words and phrases that you think are poetic—those that are highly descriptive or make comparisons, and so on.

3 In the space below, list a few of the words and phrases you underlined and explain what it was about the words that made you think they might work in your found poem. Maybe you like the sound of a word, maybe it reminds you of something, or perhaps it conjures a picture in your mind.

Words I Chose	**Why I Chose Them**
1. _____	_____
2. _____	_____
3. _____	_____
4. _____	_____
5. _____	_____
6. _____	_____

Teaching 10 Fabulous Forms of Poetry by Paul B. Janeczko   Scholastic Professional Books

Name _____ Date _____

Drafting a Found Poem

1 Copy the poetic words and phrases you found in the passage on small slips of paper. If you found individual words, write each on a separate slip of paper. If you found phrases, write the phrase.

2 Play and experiment with your slips of paper. Move them around on your desk to see what interesting, poetic arrangements you can make. You may need to add some connecting words, such as: *the, and, in, an, a.*

3 When your found poem sounds right to you, write it at the bottom of this page. This is your first draft. Then, move the slips of paper around on your desk some more and see what other arrangements you can find. Don't be afraid to try something unusual, even wild. If you find a new version of your poem, write it on another sheet of paper.

4 Give your poem a title.

_____

_____

_____

_____

_____

_____

_____

_____

_____

_____

Name _____ Date _____

Working on Line Breaks

1 When you are satisfied with your found poem, read it aloud to a friend.

2 Listen as you read it to see if you can *hear* where your lines end. Often, where you naturally pause to take a breath is a reasonable place to end a line. The end of a line should be a mini-pause, not a complete stop like you make when you come to the end of a sentence.

3 Ask your friend to comment. Write a few of these comments and suggestions here:

_____

_____

_____

_____

_____

4 Now, listen to your friend's poem and give him or her feedback.

5 Go back and look at the words on each line of your own poem. There should be a reason to have *those* words on *that* line. Do they make sense together?

6 Do you see or hear any words you should eliminate from your poem? Draw a line through any words that can be cut. Are there words that should be moved to another line? Draw an arrow to show where they should go.

7 When you have made changes to your poem and are happy with it, rewrite it on a separate sheet of paper.

Teaching 10 Fabulous Forms of Poetry by Paul B. Janeczko   Scholastic Professional Books

Final Thoughts

As I said in the introduction of this book, the poetry writing opportunities are arranged in a way that reflects something of the degree of difficulty, from simplest to more complex. It makes sense, therefore, to let your students try to write these poetic forms in that order because as they develop as writers, they will be ready to write more challenging poems. However, if you see that one of these poetic forms will fit nicely into a unit you are developing for another curriculum area, I encourage you to let your kids try it. For example, if you are doing a unit on biography, you might want your students to try writing a clerihew. Or, perhaps the haiku or the tanka would fit into a science unit on pond life. In fact, having your students write poetry for other subject areas will show them that poetry can be about all sorts of things.

I would encourage you to try these units yourself before you present them to your students. Since you know your students better that I do, such a "dry run" will give you a chance to see if you need to make modifications in a unit as I present it. Trust your instincts.

Everyone who wants to write poetry—kids and teachers alike—should read lots of poetry. The more poetry you read, the more possibilities you will see in it—and the more apt you will be to find poems that can work either as writing models or serve as additional examples of forms your kids already write.

Finally, enjoy yourself as you and your students write poetry. Be kind and constructive with your comments to your young writers. And give yourself and your kids every chance to succeed.

RECOMMENDED BOOKS
ON TEACHING POETRY WRITING

Dunning, Stephen & William Stafford. *Getting the Knack: 20 Poetry Writing Exercises.* NCTE, 1992.

Fletcher, Ralph. *Breathing In, Breathing Out.* Heinemann, 1996.

_____. *What a Writer Needs.* Heinemann, 1992.

Glover, Mary Kenner. *A Garden of Poets.* NCTE, 1999.

Graves, Donald H. *Explore Poetry.* Heinemann, 1992.

Green, Benjamin. *Beyond Roses are Red, Violets are Blue.* Cottonwood Press, 1996.

Heard, Georgia. *For the Good of Earth and Sun.* Heinemann, 1989.

_____. *Awakening the Heart: Exploring Poetry in Elementary and Middle Schools.* Heinemann, 1998.

Janeczko, Paul B. *Favorite Poetry Lessons.* Scholastic, 1998.

_____. *How to Write Poetry.* Scholastic, 1999.

_____. *Poetry From A to Z: A Guide for Young Writers.* Simon & Schuster, 1996.

Johnson, David M. *Word Weaving.* NCTE, 1990.

King, Laurie & Dennis Stoval. *Classroom Publishing.* Blue Heron Publishing, 1992.

Kennedy, X. J. & Dorothy M. Kennedy. *Knock at a Star* (revised edition). Little Brown, 1999.

Koch, Kenneth. *Making Your Own Days: The Pleasures of Reading and Writing Poetry.* Simon & Schuster, 1998.

Kohl, Herbert. *A Grain of Poetry.* HarperCollins, 1999.

Livingston, Myra Cohn. *Poem-Making: Ways to Begin Writing Poetry.* HarperCollins, 1991.

Lyon, George Ella. *Where I'm From: Where Poems Come From.* Absey & Co., 1999.

McClure, Amy A. *Sunrises and Songs: Reading and Writing Poetry in an Elementary Classroom.* Heinemann, 1990.

McVeigh-Schultz, Jane & Mary Lynn Ellis. *With a Poet's Eye.* Heinemann, 1997.

Padgett, Ron, ed. *Handbook of Poetic Forms.* Teachers & Writers Collaborative, 1987.

Routman, Regie. *Kids' Poems: Teaching Third & Fourth Graders to Love Writing Poetry.* Scholastic, 2000.

Steinbergh, Judith W. *Reading and Writing Poetry.* Scholastic, 1994.

Sweeney, Jacqueline. *Teaching Poetry: Yes You Can!* Scholastic, 1993.

Tannenbaum, Judith. *Teeth, Wiggly as Earthquakes.* Stenhouse Publishers, 2000.

Tucker, Shelley. *Painting the Sky.* Good Year Books, 1994.

_____. *Word Weavings.* Good Year Books, 1997.

Wilson, Lorraine. *Write Me a Poem.* Heinemann, 1994.

Wooldridge, Susan G. *Poemcrazy.* Clarkson Potter, 1996.